W9-CNJ-793

SCHOLASTIC

Do The Math™

Created by
Marilyn Burns

Fractions Ⓐ

Basic Concepts

....

WorkSpace

All rights reserved.   Published by Scholastic Inc.   Printed in the U.S.A.

ISBN-13: 978-0-545-00988-1
ISBN-10: 0-545-00988-X

SCHOLASTIC, DO THE MATH, and associated logos and designs are trademarks and/or registered trademarks of Scholastic Inc.

1   2   3   4   5   6   7   8   9   10   40   16   15   14   13   12   11   10   09   08   07

Fraction Relationships

1 How many $\frac{1}{8}$ equal $\frac{1}{2}$?

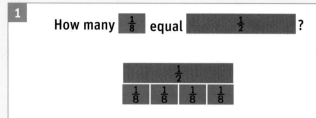

Use your fraction pieces to answer the question.

2 ___4___ eighths is equal to one-half.

Complete the sentence.

3 $\dfrac{4}{8} = \dfrac{1}{2}$

Write a fraction.

① How many $\frac{1}{4}$ equal $\frac{1}{2}$?

_____ fourths is equal to one-half.

_____ $= \dfrac{1}{2}$

Home Note: Your child combines fraction pieces to identify equivalent fractions.

② How many $\frac{1}{16}$ equal $\frac{1}{8}$ $\frac{1}{8}$?

_____ sixteenths is equal to two-eighths.

$$\frac{\rule{1cm}{0.4pt}}{} = \frac{2}{8}$$

③ How many $\frac{1}{4}$ equal $\frac{1}{8}$ $\frac{1}{8}$ $\frac{1}{8}$ $\frac{1}{8}$ $\frac{1}{8}$ $\frac{1}{8}$?

_____ fourths is equal to six-eighths.

$$\frac{\rule{1cm}{0.4pt}}{} = \frac{6}{8}$$

④ How many $\frac{1}{8}$ equal $\frac{1}{2}$ $\frac{1}{2}$?

_____ eighths is equal to two-halves.

$$\frac{\rule{1cm}{0.4pt}}{} = \frac{2}{2}$$

Home Note: Your child combines fraction pieces to identify equivalent fractions.

Game Rules for Cover Up

What you need

- fraction pieces
- fraction cube ($\frac{1}{2}$, $\frac{1}{4}$, $\frac{1}{8}$, $\frac{1}{8}$, $\frac{1}{16}$, $\frac{1}{16}$)

➤ **Start with your blue whole strip.**

➤ **Players take turns. Each turn has three steps.**

1

Roll the fraction cube.
Place the fraction piece shown
by the cube on the whole strip.

2

Your partner checks to be sure
the piece you placed is correct.

3

When you finish, say "Done"
and hand the cube to your partner.

➤ **The winner is the first player who exactly covers the whole strip.**

Home Note: Your child plays a game adding fractions with a sum of exactly 1.

Cover the Whole

DIRECTIONS

1

Make a train with your fraction pieces to cover your whole strip exactly.

2

$$\frac{1}{8} + \frac{1}{4} + \frac{1}{2} + \frac{1}{16} + \frac{1}{16} = 1$$

Write an equation.

3

$$\frac{1}{8} + \frac{1}{4} + \frac{1}{2} + \frac{2}{16} = 1$$

Shorten the equation.

---

(1) Equation

Shorten the equation.

(2) Equation

Shorten the equation.

(3) Equation

Shorten the equation.

(4) Equation

Shorten the equation.

Home Note: Your child uses fraction pieces to make an exact whole and writes equations to show the sum of the fractions.

Show What You Know

DIRECTIONS

➤ Use your fraction pieces to answer the question.

➤ Complete the sentence.

➤ Write a fraction.

1. How many $\frac{1}{8}$ equal $\frac{1}{4}$ $\frac{1}{4}$ $\frac{1}{4}$?

   _____ eighths is equal to three-fourths.

   $\underline{\hspace{1.5cm}} = \dfrac{3}{4}$

2. How many $\frac{1}{16}$ equal $\frac{1}{8}$ $\frac{1}{8}$ $\frac{1}{8}$?

   _____ sixteenths is equal to three-eighths.

   $\underline{\hspace{1.5cm}} = \dfrac{3}{8}$

3. How many $\frac{1}{8}$ equal $\frac{1}{2}$?

   _____ eighths is equal to one-half.

   $\underline{\hspace{1.5cm}} = \dfrac{1}{2}$

4. How many $\frac{1}{4}$ equal $\frac{1}{2}$ $\frac{1}{2}$?

   _____ fourths is equal to two-halves.

   $\underline{\hspace{1.5cm}} = \dfrac{2}{2}$

Home Note: Your child identifies equivalent fractions by comparing the sizes of fraction pieces.

Show What You Know

DIRECTIONS

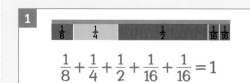

1

$$\frac{1}{8} + \frac{1}{4} + \frac{1}{2} + \frac{1}{16} + \frac{1}{16} = 1$$

Write an equation.

2

$$\frac{1}{8} + \frac{1}{4} + \frac{1}{2} + \frac{2}{16} = 1$$

Shorten the equation.

---

①

Equation

Shorten the equation.

---

②

Equation

Shorten the equation.

Home Note: Your child uses fraction pieces to make an exact whole and writes equations to show the sum of the fractions.

Game Rules for Uncover 1

What you need

- fraction pieces
- fraction cube ($\frac{1}{2}, \frac{1}{4}, \frac{1}{8}, \frac{1}{8}, \frac{1}{16}, \frac{1}{16}$)

➤ Each player covers his or her whole strip with two $\frac{1}{2}$ pieces.

➤ Each turn has 4 steps. You may not exchange and remove pieces in the same turn.

1

Roll the fraction cube.

2

You have three choices:

• Remove the piece shown on the fraction cube.

• Exchange one of the pieces for equivalent pieces.

• Do nothing.

3

Your partner checks to be sure
he or she agrees with what you did.

4

When you finish, say "Done" and hand the cube to your partner.

➤ The winner is the first player to uncover a whole strip by rolling a fraction that exactly matches the last piece on the strip.

Home Note: Your child plays a game using equivalent fractions.

Comparing Pairs

DIRECTIONS

$\dfrac{3}{8}$ ☐ $\dfrac{9}{16}$

1

Use your fraction pieces to make fraction trains.

2

$\dfrac{3}{8}$ $\boxed{<}$ $\dfrac{9}{16}$

Write <, >, or =.

① $\dfrac{3}{4}$ ☐ $\dfrac{5}{8}$

② $\dfrac{1}{4}$ ☐ $\dfrac{1}{8}$

③ $\dfrac{1}{2}$ ☐ $\dfrac{4}{8}$

④ $\dfrac{1}{8}$ ☐ $\dfrac{1}{2}$

⑤ $\dfrac{6}{16}$ ☐ $\dfrac{1}{2}$

⑥ $\dfrac{7}{16}$ ☐ $\dfrac{3}{8}$

⑦ $\dfrac{5}{8}$ ☐ $\dfrac{1}{2}$

⑧ $\dfrac{10}{16}$ ☐ $\dfrac{3}{4}$

Home Note: Your child compares fractions using the symbols <, >, and =.

Game Rules for Uncover 2

What you need

- fraction pieces
- fraction cube ($\frac{1}{2}$, $\frac{1}{4}$, $\frac{1}{8}$, $\frac{1}{8}$, $\frac{1}{16}$, $\frac{1}{16}$)

➤ **Each player covers his or her whole strip with two $\frac{1}{2}$ pieces.**

➤ **Each turn has 4 steps. You may not exchange and remove pieces in the same turn.**

1

Roll the fraction cube.

2 **You have three choices:**

- Remove one or more pieces that add up to the fraction you rolled.

- Exchange one of the pieces for equivalent pieces.

- Do nothing.

3

Your partner checks to be sure
he or she agrees with what you did.

4

When you finish, say "Done"
and hand the cube to your partner.

➤ **The winner is the first player to uncover his or her whole strip.**

   Home Note: Your child plays a game using equivalent fractions.

What's Missing?

DIRECTIONS

➤ **Write the numerator or denominator that makes the fractions equivalent.**

① $\dfrac{1}{2} = \dfrac{\square}{4}$

② $\dfrac{4}{16} = \dfrac{\square}{4}$

③ $\dfrac{1}{2} = \dfrac{\square}{16}$

④ $\dfrac{\square}{4} = \dfrac{8}{16}$

⑤ $\dfrac{3}{4} = \dfrac{\square}{8}$

⑥ $\dfrac{2}{8} = \dfrac{1}{\square}$

⑦ $\dfrac{1}{2} = \dfrac{\square}{8}$

⑧ $\dfrac{2}{16} = \dfrac{\square}{8}$

⑨ $\dfrac{3}{4} = \dfrac{\square}{16}$

⑩ $\dfrac{3}{8} = \dfrac{6}{\square}$

Home Note: Your child identifies equivalent fractions.

Show What You Know

➤ Write <, >, or =.

(1) $\dfrac{3}{8}$ ☐ $\dfrac{1}{4}$

(2) $\dfrac{1}{2}$ ☐ $\dfrac{3}{4}$

(3) $\dfrac{5}{8}$ ☐ $\dfrac{10}{16}$

(4) $\dfrac{5}{8}$ ☐ $\dfrac{1}{2}$

(5) $\dfrac{5}{16}$ ☐ $\dfrac{2}{8}$

(6) $\dfrac{12}{16}$ ☐ $\dfrac{3}{4}$

(7) $\dfrac{8}{16}$ ☐ $\dfrac{1}{2}$

(8) $\dfrac{1}{2}$ ☐ $\dfrac{3}{8}$

(9) $\dfrac{7}{8}$ ☐ $\dfrac{15}{16}$

(10) $\dfrac{1}{4}$ ☐ $\dfrac{3}{16}$

Home Note: Your child compares fractions using <, >, and =.

Show What You Know

➤ Write the numerator or denominator that makes the fractions equivalent.

(1) $\frac{3}{4} = \frac{\square}{8}$

(2) $\frac{2}{4} = \frac{\square}{8}$

(3) $\frac{1}{2} = \frac{\square}{4}$

(4) $\frac{\square}{8} = \frac{1}{4}$

(5) $\frac{\square}{8} = \frac{10}{16}$

(6) $\frac{8}{\square} = \frac{1}{2}$

(7) $\frac{3}{4} = \frac{\square}{16}$

(8) $\frac{4}{8} = \frac{1}{\square}$

(9) $\frac{2}{16} = \frac{1}{\square}$

(10) $\frac{4}{\square} = \frac{1}{4}$

Home Note: Your child identifies equivalent fractions.

Rules for Pick 2

What you need

• fraction pieces

1

Make a train of two pieces that are *not* the same color.

2

Build another train that is the same length
using pieces that are all the same color.

3

$$\frac{1}{2} + \frac{1}{8} = \frac{5}{8}$$

Write an equation.

4

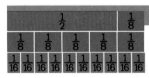

$$\frac{1}{2} + \frac{1}{8} = \frac{5}{8}$$

$$\frac{1}{2} + \frac{1}{8} = \frac{10}{16}$$

Try to build other one-color trains that have
the same length. Write an equation for each.

Home Note: Your child learns the rules of an activity in which he or she finds a fraction that
is equivalent to two combined fractions, and writes an equation showing the equivalence.

Pick 2

DIRECTIONS

➤ Follow the steps on page 14.

(1) Pick two fraction pieces _____ _____

Equations

(2) Pick two fraction pieces _____ _____

Equations

(3) Pick two fraction pieces _____ _____

Equations

(4) Pick two fraction pieces _____ _____

Equations

(5) Pick two fraction pieces _____ _____

Equations

(6) Pick two fraction pieces _____ _____

Equations

Home Note: Your child finds a fraction that is equivalent to two
combined fractions, and writes an equation showing the equivalence.

Lesson 11

15

Make a Whole

1

$\frac{1}{2}$ $\frac{1}{8}$

Place the blue whole strip. Use the fraction pieces listed to build a train.

2

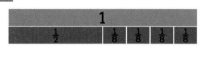

Fill the space to make a whole with pieces of one color. Do this in more than one way if possible.

3

$\frac{1}{2} + \frac{1}{8} + \frac{3}{8} = 1$

$\frac{1}{2} + \frac{1}{8} + \frac{6}{16} = 1$

Write equations.

① $\frac{1}{2}$ $\frac{1}{4}$

Equations

② $\frac{1}{4}$ $\frac{1}{8}$

Equations

③ $\frac{1}{8}$ $\frac{1}{16}$

Equations

 Home Note: Your child identifies fraction pieces to add to others to make a whole. He or she writes equations showing solutions.

(4) $\frac{1}{2}$ $\frac{1}{16}$

Equations

(5) $\frac{1}{16}$ $\frac{1}{16}$

Equations

(6) $\frac{1}{4}$ $\frac{1}{4}$

Equations

(7) $\frac{1}{4}$ $\frac{1}{16}$

Equations

(8) $\frac{1}{8}$ $\frac{1}{8}$

Equations

Home Note: Your child identifies fraction pieces to add to others to make a whole. He or she writes equations showing solutions.

Rules for Roll 5

What you need

- fraction pieces
- fraction cube ($\frac{1}{2}$, $\frac{1}{4}$, $\frac{1}{8}$, $\frac{1}{8}$, $\frac{1}{16}$, $\frac{1}{16}$)

1

 Roll: $\frac{1}{2}$ $\frac{1}{8}$ $\frac{1}{4}$ $\frac{1}{8}$ $\frac{1}{4}$

Roll the fraction cube five times. Write the fractions.
Build a train with pieces that match the fractions that you roll.

2

$$\frac{1}{2} + \frac{1}{8} + \frac{1}{4} + \frac{1}{8} + \frac{1}{4} = \boxed{}$$

$$\frac{1}{2} + \frac{2}{8} + \frac{2}{4} = \boxed{}$$

Record as shown.

3

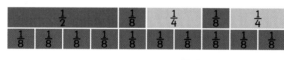

$$\frac{1}{2} + \frac{2}{8} + \frac{2}{4} = \boxed{\frac{10}{8}}$$

Build another train of equal length using pieces of one color.
Write the sum as a fraction.

4

$$\frac{1}{2} + \frac{2}{8} + \frac{2}{4} = \boxed{\frac{10}{8}} = \boxed{1\frac{2}{8}}$$

If the sum is greater than 1, write it as a mixed number.

➤ **Try to build other one-color trains that have the same
length. Write an equation for each. If the sum is greater
than 1, write it as a mixed number.**

Home Note: Your child learns the rules of an activity in which he or she builds a fraction
train from five pieces. He or she then finds an equivalent fraction and writes an equation.

Roll 5

➤ **Follow the rules on page 18.**

①

②

③

④

⑤

⑥

Home Note: Your child builds a fraction train from five pieces.
He or she then identifies an equivalent fraction and writes an equation.

Combining Fractions

1

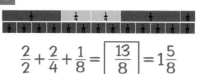

$$\frac{1}{2} + \frac{1}{4} + \frac{1}{4} + \frac{1}{2} + \frac{1}{8} = \boxed{}$$

$$\frac{2}{2} + \frac{2}{4} + \frac{1}{8} = \boxed{}$$

Build a train to match. Write an equation. Shorten the equation.

2

$$\frac{2}{2} + \frac{2}{4} + \frac{1}{8} = \boxed{\frac{13}{8}} = 1\frac{5}{8}$$

Build another train of equal length using pieces of one color. Write the sum as a fraction and as a mixed number.

3

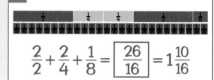

$$\frac{2}{2} + \frac{2}{4} + \frac{1}{8} = \boxed{\frac{26}{16}} = 1\frac{10}{16}$$

If possible, build other one-color trains. Write the equation with the sum as a fraction and as a mixed number.

---

① $\frac{1}{2}$ $\frac{1}{4}$ $\frac{1}{2}$ $\frac{1}{8}$ $\frac{1}{8}$

② $\frac{1}{2}$ $\frac{1}{16}$ $\frac{1}{16}$ $\frac{1}{4}$ $\frac{1}{16}$ $\frac{1}{16}$ $\frac{1}{8}$

③ $\frac{1}{16}$ $\frac{1}{4}$ $\frac{1}{2}$ $\frac{1}{4}$ $\frac{1}{16}$

 **Home Note:** Your child builds fraction trains and identifies fractions equivalent to the combined fractions.

Roll 5

DIRECTIONS

➤ Follow the rules on page 18.

①

②

③

④

⑤

⑥

Home Note: Your child builds a fraction train from five pieces.
He or she then identifies equivalent fractions and writes equations.

Show What You Know

1

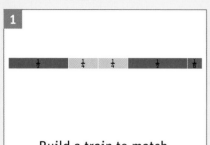

Build a train to match.

2

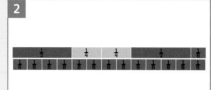

Build a train of equal length using pieces of one color.

3

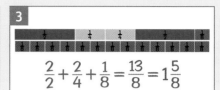

$$\frac{2}{2} + \frac{2}{4} + \frac{1}{8} = \frac{13}{8} = 1\frac{5}{8}$$

Write a shortened equation and write the sum as a fraction and, if possible, as a mixed number.

①

②

③

Lesson 15

Home Note: Your child builds fraction trains and identifies fractions equivalent to the combined fractions.

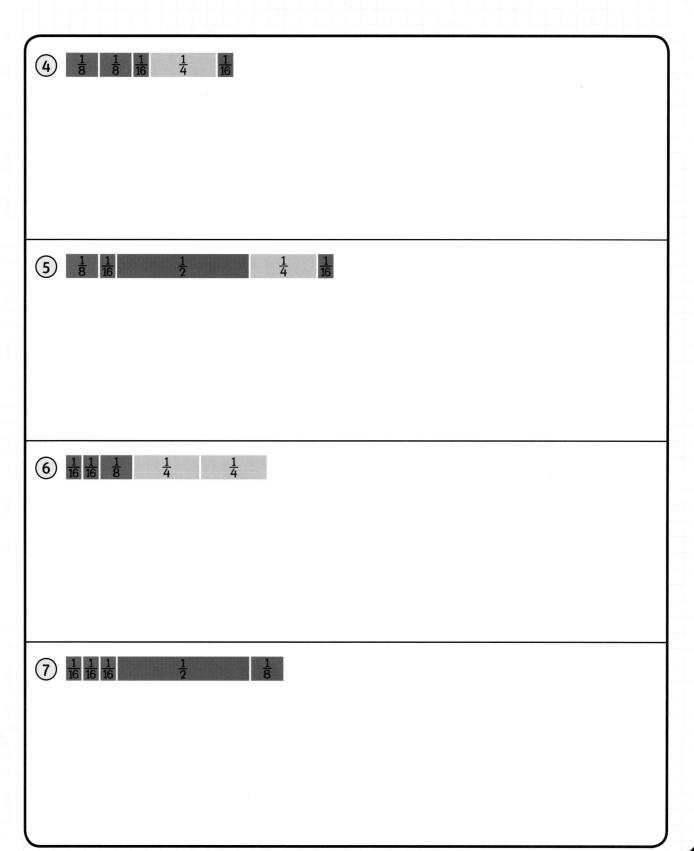

④ $\frac{1}{8}$ $\frac{1}{8}$ $\frac{1}{16}$ $\frac{1}{4}$ $\frac{1}{16}$

⑤ $\frac{1}{8}$ $\frac{1}{16}$ $\frac{1}{2}$ $\frac{1}{4}$ $\frac{1}{16}$

⑥ $\frac{1}{16}$ $\frac{1}{16}$ $\frac{1}{8}$ $\frac{1}{4}$ $\frac{1}{4}$

⑦ $\frac{1}{16}$ $\frac{1}{16}$ $\frac{1}{16}$ $\frac{1}{2}$ $\frac{1}{8}$

Home Note: Your child builds fraction trains and identifies fractions equivalent to the combined fractions.

4 People Share 4 Cookies Equally

DIRECTIONS

1 4 People Share 4 Cookies

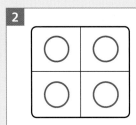

Read the title. Take that number of cookies.

2

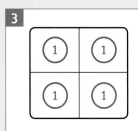

Share the cookies equally.

3

Paste and label the cookies.

4 Each person gets
1 cookie .

Record each person's share.

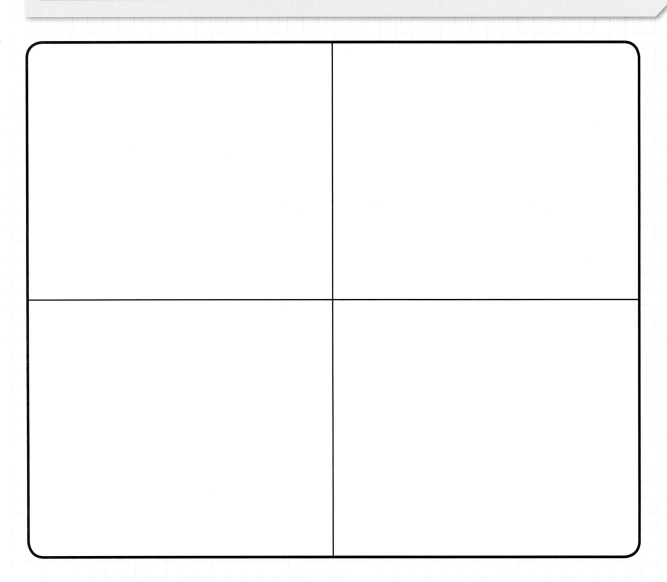

Each person gets _____ .

24 Lesson 16

Home Note: Your child uses paper circles to solve problems that involve dividing cookies into fractional parts.

4 People Share 5 Cookies Equally

DIRECTIONS

1 **4 People Share 4 Cookies**

◯ ◯ ◯ ◯

Read the title. Take that number of cookies.

2

Share the cookies equally.

3

Paste and label the cookies.

4 Each person gets
__1 cookie__ .

Record each person's share.

Each person gets _____.

Home Note: Your child uses paper circles to solve problems that involve dividing cookies into fractional parts.

4 People Share 1 Cookie Equally

1 **4 People Share 4 Cookies**

Read the title. Take that number of cookies.

2

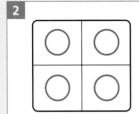

Share the cookies equally.

3

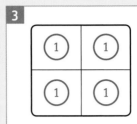

Paste and label the cookies.

4

Each person gets _____1 cookie_____ .

Record each person's share.

Each person gets _____ .

Home Note: Your child uses paper circles to solve problems that involve dividing cookies into fractional parts.

4 People Share 3 Cookies Equally

DIRECTIONS

1
4 People Share 4 Cookies

Read the title.
Take that number
of cookies.

2

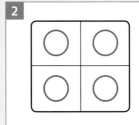

Share the
cookies equally.

3

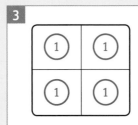

Paste and label
the cookies.

4

Each person gets
___1 cookie___.

Record each
person's share.

Each person gets _____.

 Home Note: Your child uses paper circles to solve problems
that involve dividing cookies into fractional parts.

4 People Share 2 Cookies Equally

DIRECTIONS

1
4 People Share 4 Cookies

Read the title.
Take that number
of cookies.

2

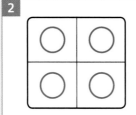

Share the
cookies equally.

3

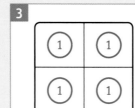

Paste and label
the cookies.

4

Each person gets
__1 cookie__ .

Record each
person's share.

Each person gets _____ .

Lesson 17

Home Note: Your child uses paper circles to solve problems
that involve dividing cookies into fractional parts.

4 People Share 6 Cookies Equally

1 **4 People Share 4 Cookies**

Read the title. Take that number of cookies.

2

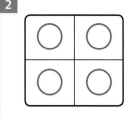

Share the cookies equally.

3

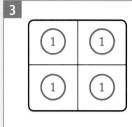

Paste and label the cookies.

4

Each person gets

1 cookie .

Record each person's share.

Each person gets _____.

 Home Note: Your child uses paper circles to solve problems that involve dividing cookies into fractional parts.

8 People Share 1 Cookie Equally

1

4 People Share 4 Cookies

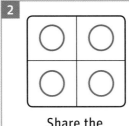

Read the title. Take that number of cookies.

2

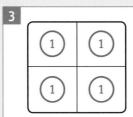

Share the cookies equally.

3

Paste and label the cookies.

4

Each person gets ___1 cookie___ .

Record each person's share.

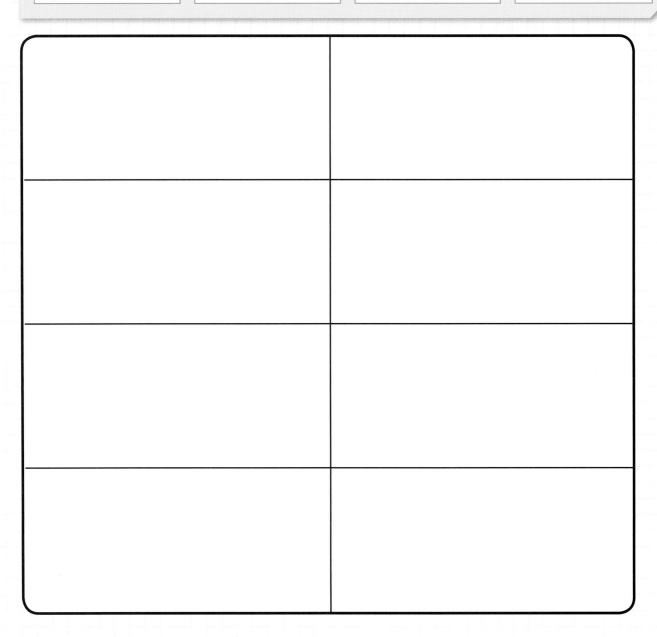

Each person gets _____ .

Lesson 18

Home Note: Your child uses paper circles to solve problems that involve dividing cookies into fractional parts.

8 People Share 3 Cookies Equally

DIRECTIONS

1 **4 People Share 4 Cookies**

Read the title. Take that number of cookies.

2 Share the cookies equally.

3 Paste and label the cookies.

4 Each person gets _1 cookie_ .

Record each person's share.

Each person gets _____.

Home Note: Your child uses paper circles to solve problems that involve dividing cookies into fractional parts.

8 People Share 4 Cookies Equally

1 **4 People Share 4 Cookies**

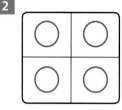

Read the title.
Take that number
of cookies.

2

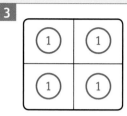

Share the
cookies equally.

3

Paste and label
the cookies.

4

Each person gets
_____1 cookie_____.

Record each
person's share.

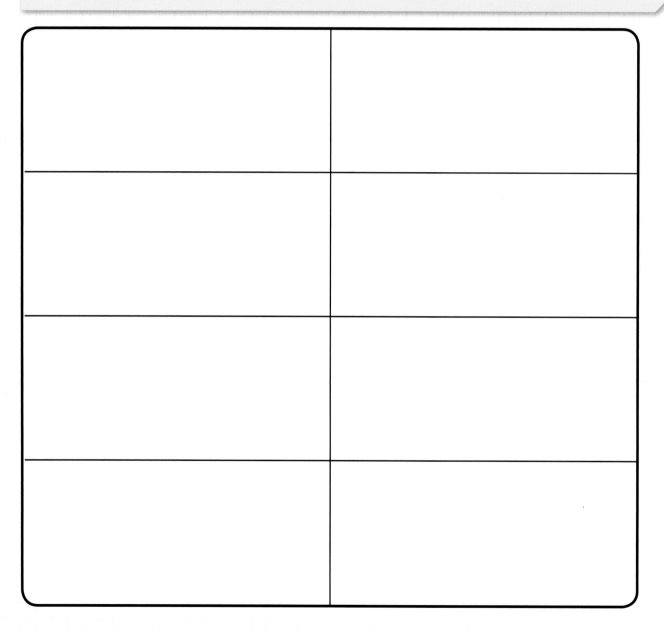

Each person gets _____.

Home Note: Your child uses paper circles to solve problems
that involve dividing cookies into fractional parts.

8 People Share 6 Cookies Equally

DIRECTIONS

1 **4 People Share 4 Cookies**

◯ ◯ ◯ ◯

Read the title. Take that number of cookies.

2

Share the cookies equally.

3

Paste and label the cookies.

4

Each person gets
1 cookie .

Record each person's share.

Each person gets _____.

 Home Note: Your child uses paper circles to solve problems that involve dividing cookies into fractional parts.

Lesson 18

33

Who Has More?

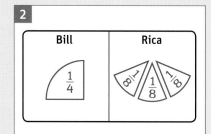

1 Bill has $\frac{1}{4}$ of a cookie.

Rica has $\frac{3}{8}$ of a cookie.

Cut cookies as needed.

2

Bill	Rica

Paste and label the cookies.

3 Who has more? ___Rica___

How do you know?

$\frac{1}{4}$ equals $\frac{2}{8}$, so $\frac{3}{8}$ is more than $\frac{1}{4}$.

Answer the questions.

---

1 Maria has $\frac{1}{2}$ of a cookie. Jeremy has $\frac{3}{4}$ of a cookie.

Maria	Jeremy

Who has more? _____ How do you know? _____

_____

2 José has $1\frac{1}{4}$ cookies. Shelly has $\frac{3}{2}$ cookies.

José	Shelly

Who has more? _____ How do you know? _____

_____

Home Note: Your child compares fractions.

③ Mia has $\frac{3}{4}$ of a cookie. Roberto has $\frac{7}{8}$ of a cookie.

Mia	Roberto

Who has more? _____

How do you know? _____

_____

④ Mike has $\frac{5}{4}$ cookies. Elena has $1\frac{3}{8}$ cookies.

Mike	Elena

Who has more? _____

How do you know? _____

_____

Home Note: Your child compares fractions.

Show What You Know

➤ Share 7 cookies equally among 4 people.

➤ Decide how many cookies go in each space. Paste them.

➤ Label the cookies.

➤ Fill in the blank.

Each person gets _____.

Lesson 20

Home Note: Your child uses paper circles to solve problems that involve dividing cookies into fractional parts.

Show What You Know

DIRECTIONS

➤ Share 2 cookies equally among 8 people.

➤ Decide how many cookies go in each space. Paste them.

➤ Label the cookies.

➤ Fill in the blank.

Each person gets _____ .

 Home Note: Your child uses paper circles to solve problems that involve dividing cookies into fractional parts.

Show What You Know

➤ Take the number of cookies. Cut them as needed.

➤ Paste the cookies in the spaces and label them.

➤ Answer the questions.

Jafar has $\frac{3}{4}$ of a cookie. Nani has $\frac{5}{8}$ of a cookie.

Jafar	Nani

Who has more? _____

How do you know? _____

_____

Home Note: Your child compares fractions.

Show What You Know

DIRECTIONS

➤ Take the number of cookies. Cut them as needed.

➤ Paste the cookies in the spaces and label them.

➤ Answer the questions.

Kiko has $1\frac{1}{2}$ cookies. Jason has $\frac{5}{4}$ cookies.

Kiko	Jason

Who has more? _____

How do you know? _____

_____

Home Note: Your child compares fractions.

A Game of Cover Up

Player A	Player B

(1) **Player A won. Write Player A's fractions as an equation.**

(2) **Write Player B's fractions.**

(3) **Use your fraction strips to identify fractions that would cover the rest of Player B's whole strip. Write the equation that has a sum of 1.**

Home Note: Your child records the results of a fraction game, and identifies the fraction or fractions needed to make a whole.

Game Rules for Cover Up

What you need

- fraction pieces
- fraction cube ($\frac{1}{2}$, $\frac{1}{3}$, $\frac{1}{4}$, $\frac{1}{6}$, $\frac{1}{12}$, $\frac{1}{12}$)

➤ **Start with your blue whole strip.**

➤ **Players take turns. Each turn has three steps.**

1

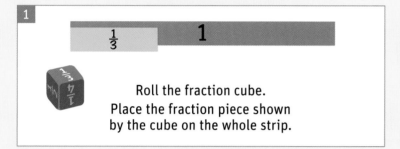

Roll the fraction cube.
Place the fraction piece shown
by the cube on the whole strip.

2

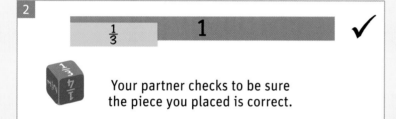

Your partner checks to be sure
the piece you placed is correct.

3

When you finish, say "Done"
and hand the cube to your partner.

➤ **The winner is the first player who exactly covers the whole strip.**

Home Note: Your child plays a game adding fractions with a sum of exactly 1.

Game Rules for Uncover 1

What you need

- fraction pieces
- fraction cube ($\frac{1}{2}$, $\frac{1}{3}$, $\frac{1}{4}$, $\frac{1}{6}$, $\frac{1}{12}$, $\frac{1}{12}$)

➤ **Each player covers his or her whole strip with two $\frac{1}{2}$ pieces.**

➤ **Each turn has 4 steps. You may not exchange and remove pieces in the same turn.**

1

Roll the fraction cube.

2 **You have three choices:**

- Remove the piece shown on the fraction cube.

- Exchange one of the pieces for equivalent pieces.

- Do nothing.

3

Your partner checks to be sure
he or she agrees with what you did.

4

When you finish, say "Done"
and hand the cube to your partner.

➤ **The winner is the first player to uncover a whole strip by rolling a fraction that exactly matches the last piece on the strip.**

Lesson 23   **Home Note:** Your child plays a game using equivalent fractions.

Game Rules for Uncover 2

What you need

• fraction pieces
• fraction cube ($\frac{1}{2}$, $\frac{1}{3}$, $\frac{1}{4}$, $\frac{1}{6}$, $\frac{1}{12}$, $\frac{1}{12}$)

➤ Each player covers his or her whole strip with two $\frac{1}{2}$ pieces.

➤ Each turn has 4 steps. You may not exchange and remove pieces in the same turn.

1

Roll the fraction cube.

2   **You have three choices:**

• Remove one or more pieces that add up to the fraction you rolled.

• Exchange one of the pieces for equivalent pieces.

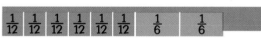

• Do nothing and pass the cube to your partner.

3

 ✓

Your partner checks to be sure
he or she agrees with what you did.

4

When you finish, say "Done"
and hand the cube to your partner.

➤ The winner is the first player to uncover a whole strip.

 Home Note: Your child plays a game using equivalent fractions.

Record Equivalent Fractions

DIRECTIONS

1 $\frac{1}{6} =$ $\boxed{\frac{1}{6}}$ Take the piece.	**2** $\boxed{\frac{1}{6}}$ $\boxed{\frac{1}{12}}\ \boxed{\frac{1}{12}}$ Make a one-color train the same length.	**3** $\frac{1}{6} = \frac{2}{12}$ Write an equation.

Use these pieces.

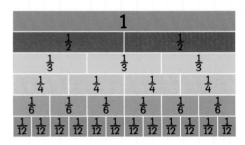

① $\frac{1}{6} =$

② $\frac{1}{4} =$

③ $\frac{1}{3} =$

④ $\frac{1}{2} =$

⑤ $1 =$

Home Note: Your child completes equations to identify equivalent fractions.

Rules for Pick 2

What you need

- fraction pieces

1

Make a train of two pieces
that are *not* the same color.

2

Build another train that is the same length
using pieces that are all the same color.

3

$$\frac{1}{4} + \frac{1}{12} = \frac{4}{12}$$

Write an equation.

4

$$\frac{1}{4} + \frac{1}{12} = \frac{4}{12}$$

$$\frac{1}{4} + \frac{1}{12} = \frac{2}{6}$$

$$\frac{1}{4} + \frac{1}{12} = \frac{1}{3}$$

Try to build other one-color trains that have
the same length. Write an equation for each.

Home Note: Your child learns the rules of an activity in which he or she identifies a fraction
that is equivalent to two combined fractions, and writes an equation showing the equivalence.

Pick 2

DIRECTIONS

➤ Use your fraction pieces for 1, $\frac{1}{2}$, $\frac{1}{3}$, $\frac{1}{4}$, $\frac{1}{6}$, and $\frac{1}{12}$.

➤ Follow the directions on page 45.

①

②

③

④

⑤

⑥

Lesson 24

Home Note: Your child identifies a fraction that is equivalent to two combined fractions, and writes an equation showing the equivalence.

Show What You Know

DIRECTIONS

➤ Write the numerators that make the fractions equivalent.

① $1 = \dfrac{\square}{3}$

② $\dfrac{1}{2} = \dfrac{\square}{6}$

③ $\dfrac{1}{4} = \dfrac{\square}{12}$

④ $\dfrac{2}{3} = \dfrac{\square}{6}$

⑤ $\dfrac{9}{12} = \dfrac{\square}{4}$

⑥ $\dfrac{8}{12} = \dfrac{\square}{3}$

Home Note: Your child uses fraction pieces to identify equivalent fractions.

Show What You Know

 1

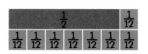

Build a one-color train that is the same length.

 2

$\frac{1}{2} + \frac{1}{12} = \underline{\frac{7}{12}}$

Write the sum.

---

① $\frac{1}{2}$ $\frac{1}{3}$

$\frac{1}{2} + \frac{1}{3} = \underline{\hspace{1cm}}$

---

② $\frac{1}{3}$ $\frac{1}{6}$

$\frac{1}{3} + \frac{1}{6} = \underline{\hspace{1cm}}$

---

③ $\frac{1}{4}$ $\frac{1}{12}$

$\frac{1}{4} + \frac{1}{12} = \underline{\hspace{1cm}}$

Home Note: Your child uses fraction pieces to identify fractions that are equivalent to two combined fractions.

3 People Share 1 Cookie Equally

DIRECTIONS

➤ Read the title. Take that number of cookies.

➤ Share the cookies equally.

➤ Paste and label the cookies.

➤ Record each person's share.

Each person gets _____ .

Home Note: Your child uses paper circles to solve problems that involve dividing cookies into fractional parts.

3 People Share 2 Cookies Equally

DIRECTIONS

➤ Read the title. Take that number of cookies.

➤ Share the cookies equally.

➤ Paste and label the cookies.

➤ Record each person's share.

Each person gets _____.

Lesson 26

Home Note: Your child uses paper circles to solve problems that involve dividing cookies into fractional parts.

3 People Share 4 Cookies Equally

DIRECTIONS

➤ Read the title. Take that number of cookies.

➤ Share the cookies equally.

➤ Paste and label the cookies.

➤ Record each person's share.

Each person gets _____ .

 Home Note: Your child uses paper circles to solve problems that involve dividing cookies into fractional parts.

3 People Share 8 Cookies Equally

DIRECTIONS

➤ Read the title. Take that number of cookies.

➤ Share the cookies equally.

➤ Paste and label the cookies.

➤ Record each person's share.

Each person gets _____.

Home Note: Your child uses paper circles to solve problems
that involve dividing cookies into fractional parts.

Comparing Fractions to $\frac{1}{2}$

➤ Write each fraction in the correct column of the table.

$\frac{1}{8}$, $\frac{7}{8}$, $\frac{4}{6}$, $\frac{1}{4}$, $\frac{3}{2}$, $\frac{5}{8}$, $\frac{3}{16}$, $\frac{5}{12}$, $\frac{3}{4}$, $\frac{4}{3}$, $\frac{9}{16}$, $\frac{2}{6}$

$< \frac{1}{2}$	$= \frac{1}{2}$	$> \frac{1}{2}$

Home Note: Your child compares fractions to $\frac{1}{2}$, using $<$, $>$, or $=$.

Put in Order

➤ Write the fractions $\frac{6}{6}$, $\frac{1}{2}$, $\frac{13}{12}$ in the cards, from least to greatest.

➤ Draw a card for $\frac{3}{4}$ so that the fractions are still in order.

➤ Explain why you put $\frac{3}{4}$ where you did. You may use words, pictures, or numbers.

①

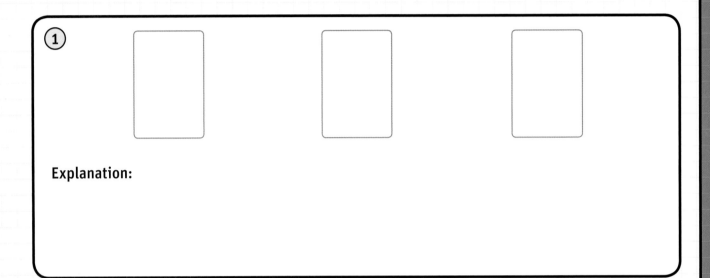

Explanation:

➤ Write the fractions $\frac{3}{4}$, $\frac{4}{3}$, $\frac{1}{2}$ in the cards, from least to greatest.

➤ Explain how you decided the order. You may use words, pictures, or numbers.

②

Explanation:

 Home Note: Your child writes fractions in order from least to greatest.

Write About Fractions

> ➤ Tell about fractions with words, numbers, and pictures.

ABOUT FRACTIONS

Home Note: Your child communicates what he or she knows about fractions.

Show What You Know
3 People Share 5 Cookies Equally

DIRECTIONS

➤ Read the title. Take that number of cookies.

➤ Share the cookies equally.

➤ Paste and label the cookies.

➤ Record each person's share.

Each person gets _____.

Lesson 30

Home Note: Your child uses paper circles to solve problems that involve dividing cookies into fractional parts.

Show What You Know

➤ Write each fraction in the correct column of the table.

$$\frac{1}{6}, \frac{5}{4}, \frac{2}{4}, \frac{3}{8}, \frac{11}{12}$$

$< \frac{1}{2}$	$= \frac{1}{2}$	$> \frac{1}{2}$

➤ Write the fractions $\frac{1}{2}$, $\frac{5}{12}$, and $\frac{5}{6}$ in order from least to greatest.

➤ Explain how you determined the order.

_____ _____ _____

Explanation: _____

_____

_____

Home Note: Your child compares fractions to $\frac{1}{2}$ and orders unlike fractions.

Math Vocabulary

➤ Write new words in the box.

➤ Write a definition, show an example, or draw a picture for each word in your list.

Math Vocabulary

Home Note: Your child reinforces his or her understanding of fractions as he or she records terms and examples.

Math Vocabulary, continued

Home Note: Your child reinforces his or her understanding
of fractions as he or she records terms and examples.

Glossary

denominator

The number below the fraction bar in a fraction is called the *denominator*. It tells how many equal parts are in the whole. 4 is the *denominator* in $\frac{3}{4}$. In $\frac{3}{4}$, 4 indicates that the whole is divided into four equal parts. The example shows three out of four colored green.

Whole divided into 4 equal parts:

equal

Equal means the same amount. For example, two-eighths equals one-fourth. The symbol for equals is =. $\frac{2}{8} = \frac{1}{4}$

equation

An *equation* is a number sentence that uses an equal sign to show that two amounts have the same value. $\frac{1}{4} + \frac{1}{4} = \frac{1}{2}$ is an equation.

equivalent

Equivalent fractions are fractions that have the same or equal value. $\frac{2}{4}$ equals $\frac{1}{2}$ so, $\frac{2}{4}$ and $\frac{1}{2}$ are equivalent.

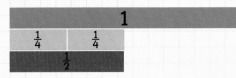

fraction

Fractions are numbers that name parts of a whole.

$\frac{5}{8}$ is a *fraction* that means 5 out of 8 equal parts.

$\frac{5}{8}$ of a whole

fraction bar

A *fraction bar* is the line that separates the numerator and the denominator of a fraction.

In $\frac{3}{4}$ the red line is the fraction bar.

improper fraction

In an *improper fraction*, the numerator is greater than the denominator. An improper fraction is always greater than 1. $\frac{3}{2}$ is an improper fraction.

mixed number

A number is called a *mixed number* when part of it is a whole number and another part is a fraction. For example $1\frac{1}{4}$ is a *mixed number* because it has a whole number 1 and a fraction $\frac{1}{4}$. $1\frac{1}{4}$ is another way to write $\frac{5}{4}$.

numerator

Numerator is the name for the number above the fraction bar in a fraction. 3 is the *numerator* in $\frac{3}{4}$.

It tells how many of the equal parts are being described. In $\frac{3}{4}$, the 3 tells you 3 parts out of a total of 4 equal parts.

3 parts of 4 equal parts are colored green. $\frac{3}{4}$ is green.

one-eighth or $\frac{1}{8}$

One-eighth is how you read $\frac{1}{8}$. It is a fraction and means one out of eight equal parts.

If you divide a whole into 8 equal parts, one of the parts is *one-eighth* of the whole.

 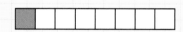

one-fourth or $\frac{1}{4}$

One-fourth is how you read $\frac{1}{4}$. It is a fraction and means one out of four equal parts.

If you divide a whole into 4 equal parts, one of the parts is *one-fourth* of the whole.

 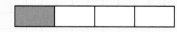

one-half or $\frac{1}{2}$

One-half is how you read $\frac{1}{2}$. It is a fraction and means one out of two equal parts.

If you divide a whole into 2 equal parts, one of the parts is *one-half* of the whole.

one-quarter or $\frac{1}{4}$

This is another way to say one-fourth (see *one-fourth*).

one-sixteenth or $\frac{1}{16}$

One-sixteenth is how you read $\frac{1}{16}$. It is a fraction and means one out of sixteen equal parts.

If you divide a whole into 16 equal parts, one of the parts is *one-sixteenth* of the whole.

 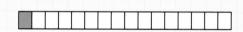

one-sixth or $\frac{1}{6}$

One-sixth is how you read $\frac{1}{6}$. It is a fraction and means one out of eight equal parts.

If you divide a whole into 6 equal parts, one of the parts is *one-sixth* of the whole.

 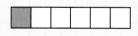

Glossary

one-third or $\frac{1}{3}$

One-third is how you read $\frac{1}{3}$. It is a fraction and means one out of three equal parts.

If you divide a whole into 3 equal parts, one of the parts is *one-third* of the whole.

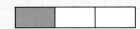

one-twelfth or $\frac{1}{12}$

One-twelfth is how you read $\frac{1}{12}$. It is a fraction and means one out of twelve equal parts.

If you divide a whole into 12 equal parts, one of the parts is *one-twelfth* of the whole.

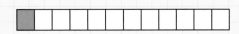

symbols

You use *symbols* in mathematics to name numbers (12, 308, $\frac{1}{2}$), operations (+, −, ×, ÷), and relationships between numbers (=, >, <, ≈).

- **=** stands for *equals*. For example, we read $\frac{1}{4} = \frac{2}{8}$ as one-fourth equals two-eighths.

- **>** stands for *is greater than*. For example, we read $\frac{3}{4} > \frac{1}{2}$ as three-fourths is greater than one-half.

- **<** stands for *is less than*. For example, we read $\frac{1}{4} < \frac{1}{2}$ as one-fourth is less than one-half.

- **≈** stands for *is about or close to*. For example, we read $\frac{7}{8} \approx 1$ as seven-eighths is about 1 or close to 1.

whole

When you say $\frac{1}{4}$, you are talking about $\frac{1}{4}$ of a *whole*. It is important to know what the *whole* is because the whole determines the size of the fractional parts. For example, it is important to know the *whole* with pizzas because $\frac{1}{4}$ of a small pizza is less than $\frac{1}{4}$ of a large pizza. When you use your fraction strips, the *whole* is the dark blue strip and all of the other fraction strips are fractional parts of that *whole*.

Here are two wholes each divided into fractional parts. Each part is $\frac{1}{4}$.

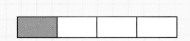